Good Housekeeping

Chocolate

HEARST BOOKS

A Division of Sterling Publishing Co., Inc.

New York

Ellen Levine   Editor in Chief
Susan Westmoreland   Food Director
Susan Deborah Goldsmith   Associate Food Director
Delia Hammock   Nutrition Director
Sharon Franke   Food Appliances Director
Richard Eisenberg   Special Projects Director
Marilu Lopez   Design Director

2   4   6   8   10   9   7   5   3   1

Book design by Liz Trovato

Photography Credits
Sang An: Page 27
Peter Ardito: Page 23
Rita Maas: Pages 1, 8, 16, 24, 29
Steven Mark Needham: Page 7, 12
Alan Richardson: Pages 19, 20
Ann Stratton: Page 15
Mark Thomas: Pages 3, 11

Published by Hearst Books
A Division of Sterling Publishing Co., Inc.
387 Park Avenue South, New York, NY 10016

The recipes in this book have been excerpted from *Chocolate! Good Housekeeping Favorite Recipes.*

Good Housekeeping is a trademark owned by Hearst Magazines Property, Inc., in USA,
and Hearst Communications, Inc., in Canada. Hearst Books is a trademark owned by
Hearst Communications, Inc.

The Good Housekeeping Cookbook Seal guarantees that the recipes in this cookbook meet the
strict standards of the Good Housekeeping Institute, a source of reliable information and a consumer advocate since 1900.
Every recipe has been triple-tested for ease, reliability, and great taste.

www.goodhousekeeping.com

Distributed in Canada by Sterling Publishing
c/o Canadian Manda Group, 165 Dufferin Street
Toronto, Ontario, Canada M6K 3H6
Distributed in Australia by Capricorn Link (Australia) Pty. Ltd.
P.O. Box 704, Windsor, NSW 2756 Australia

Manufactured in China

ISBN 1-58816-542-6

Contents

Chocolate—"Food of the Gods"

This book is for chocolate lovers who covet rich, fudgy desserts. Our recipes are a collection of unabashedly rich, tempting, and sometimes downright decadent ways to enjoy chocolate, the "food of the gods." For many of us, a day without a chocolate treat is a day without sunshine; while for others, chocolate is a greatly anticipated and slowly savored occasional indulgence. Our intent is to deliver chocolate at its very best. All of our recipes are written in the easy-to-follow, step-by-step *Good Housekeeping* style, so they will turn out perfect time after time, whether you are just learning your way around the kitchen or can "cook with your eyes closed."

How Chocolate Is Made

In a way chocolate *does* grow on trees, the cacao tree, whose botanical name is *Theobroma cacao*, from the Greek for "food of the gods." Cacao trees need three things to thrive: high temperature, high humidity, and a special insect that pollinates its flowers. The flowers that do not produce fruit develop large pods that contain cocoa beans. The beans are removed from the pods and placed in piles to ferment, after which they are left in the sun to dry. The cocoa beans are then roasted and their papery husks removed by gently crushing the beans into little, irregular pieces known as nibs. The nibs are ground, and the fat they contain—cocoa butter—is then liquefied. The whole mixture is turned into a mass called chocolate liquor, which despite its name is a solid and does not contain alcohol. The chocolate liquor is then used to make cocoa and chocolate for all the world to enjoy.

Types of Chocolate

Unsweetened chocolate is simply ground cocoa beans. Professionals call it chocolate liquor. It is harsh and bitter tasting and is never eaten out of hand. It is most often used in baking in combination with semisweet chocolate

Bittersweet chocolate has been sweetened, but the amount of sugar varies from brand to brand. Some bittersweet chocolates list the percentage of chocolate liquor: a chocolate with 70 percent is more bitter and has a more intense flavor than one with 64 percent.

Semisweet chocolate is similar to bittersweet chocolate, although it is usually a bit sweeter. It can be used interchangeably with bittersweet chocolate in most recipes. It is available in 1-ounce squares, in small bars, and in bulk at specialty food stores.

German's sweet chocolate, used to make German chocolate cake, is sold under a brand name and should not be confused with bittersweet or semisweet chocolate.

Milk chocolate contains dried milk powder and a high percentage of sugar. It is essentially an eating chocolate—it's not usually used for baking.

White chocolate is not really chocolate at all but rather vanilla-flavored sweetened cocoa butter (a by-product of chocolate processing), although some mid-priced brands substitute vegetable fat for the cocoa butter.

Unsweetened cocoa is what provides the rich chocolate flavor in many desserts. There are two kinds of cocoa powder: natural and Dutch-process. In baking, the two are not interchangeable. Natural cocoa has a full, rich flavor and is the type most commonly used in American kitchens. It is always combined with baking soda. Dutch-process cocoa is treated with an alkalai that reduces its acidity. It gives baked goods a rich dark color and it doesn't need to be combined with baking soda. For a hot cup of cocoa, use your favorite.

Chocolate Basics

Storing Chocolate Chocolate is best stored in a cool, dry place, such as a pantry. Or wrap the chocolate in an airtight heavy plastic bag and place in the crisper drawer of your refrigerator. To prevent the chocolate from developing condensation, let it come to room temperature while still wrapped before chopping or breaking it up. If chocolate is stored at warmer temperatures, it may develop a "bloom" (the cocoa butter rising to the surface), which are grayish streaks. Chocolate that has developed a bloom is perfectly fine to melt and use in cooking or baking.

Chopping Chocolate Use a large chef's knife or heavy serrated knife to cut chocolate into pieces. Be sure to use a perfectly clean and dry cutting board. To finely chop chocolate, cut it into small pieces (about 1/4 inch) by hand, then pulse it in a food processor fitted with the metal blade until finely chopped.

Melting Chocolate There is a simple rule when it comes to melting chocolate: keep the heat low and the chocolate dry. Even one tiny drop of water can cause the chocolate to "seize up" (stiffen), which ruins it. There are two easy ways to melt chocolate: in the microwave or in a double boiler or bowl set over simmering water. It is not a good idea to melt chocolate in a saucepan unless the chocolate is combined with other ingredients such as cream or butter and the saucepan is heavy.

Before melting chocolate, always chop or break it into little pieces (about 1/4 inch) so it can melt quickly and evenly. To melt chocolate on the stovetop place it in a bowl on top of a double boiler set over—not in—a pan containing about 1 1/2 inches of simmering water set over low heat. Stir occasionally with a heat-safe spatula until the chocolate is melted and smooth, then set the bowl on the counter. To melt chocolate in a microwave, place the chopped chocolate in a microwave-safe bowl. Heat it on Low or Medium-Low power at 30-second intervals, stirring, to see if the chocolate has melted. When chocolate is melted in the microwave, it continues to hold its shape even when melted.

Classic Devil's Food Cake

Devil's food cake is a twentieth-century creation. No one knows for sure how the cake got its name, but many believe it was due to its dark color and richness—the opposite of light and delicate angel food cake.

2	cups all-purpose flour
1	cup unsweetened cocoa
1 1/2	teaspoons baking soda
1/2	teaspoon salt
1/2	cup butter or margarine (1 stick), softened
1	cup packed light brown sugar
1	cup granulated sugar
3	large eggs
1 1/2	teaspoons vanilla extract
1 1/2	cups buttermilk
	Rich Chocolate Frosting (recipe follows)

• Preheat oven to 350°F. Grease three 8-inch round cake pans. Line bottoms with waxed paper; grease paper. Dust pans with flour.

• In medium bowl, combine flour, cocoa, baking soda, and salt.

• In large bowl, with mixer at low speed, beat butter and brown and granulated sugars until blended. Increase speed to high; beat until light and fluffy, about 5 minutes. Reduce speed to medium-low; add eggs, one at a time, beating well after each addition. Beat in vanilla. Add flour mixture alternately with buttermilk, beginning and ending with flour mixture; beat just until batter is smooth, occasionally scraping bowl with rubber spatula.

• Divide batter equally among prepared pans; spread evenly. Place two pans on upper oven rack and one pan on lower oven rack so pans are not directly above one another. Bake until toothpick inserted in center comes out clean, 30 to 35 minutes. Cool layers in pans on wire rack 10 minutes. Run thin knife around layers to loosen from sides of pans. Invert onto racks. Remove waxed paper; cool completely.

• Meanwhile, prepare Rich Chocolate Frosting. Place one cake layer, rounded side down, on cake plate. With narrow metal spatula, spread 1/3 cup frosting over layer. Top with second layer, rounded side up, and spread 1/3 cup frosting over layer. Place remaining layer, rounded side up, on top. Spread remaining frosting over side and top of cake.

Each serving: About 450 calories, 5g protein, 74g carbohydrate, 17g total fat (10g saturated), 72mg cholesterol, 355mg sodium.

Rich Chocolate Frosting

PREP 15 MINUTES   MAKES ABOUT 2¹/₂ CUPS

4   squares (4 ounces) semisweet chocolate

2   squares (2 ounces) unsweetened chocolate

2   cups confectioners' sugar

3/4   cup butter or margarine (1¹/2 sticks), softened

1   teaspoon vanilla extract

• In heavy 1-quart saucepan, melt semisweet and unsweetened chocolates over low heat, stirring frequently, until smooth. Remove from heat; cool to room temperature.

• In large bowl, with mixer at low speed, beat confectioners' sugar, butter, and vanilla until almost combined. Add melted chocolates. Increase speed to high; beat until light and fluffy, about 1 minute.

Each tablespoon: About 75 calories, 0g protein, 8g carbohydrate, 6g total fat (3g saturated), 9mg cholesterol, 36mg sodium.

Fabulous Flourless Chocolate Cake

PREP 1 HOUR PLUS OVERNIGHT TO CHILL   BAKE 35 MINUTES   MAKES 20 SERVINGS

This exceptionally sinful chocolate dessert is easy to make, but it must be refrigerated for twenty-four hours before serving for the best flavor and texture. For the neatest slices, dip the knife into hot water before cutting each one.

14   squares (14 ounces) semisweet chocolate, chopped

2   squares (2 ounces) unsweetened chocolate, chopped

1   cup butter (2 sticks; do not use margarine)

9   large eggs, separated

1/2   cup granulated sugar

1/4   teaspoon cream of tartar

confectioners' sugar

• Preheat oven to 300°F. Remove bottom of 9" by 3" springform pan; cover with foil, wrapping foil around back. Replace pan bottom. Grease and flour foil bottom and side of pan.

• In heavy 2-quart saucepan, melt semisweet and unsweetened chocolates and butter over low heat, stirring frequently, until smooth. Pour chocolate mixture into large bowl.

• In small bowl, with mixer at high speed, beat egg yolks and granulated sugar until very thick and lemon-colored, about 10 minutes. With rubber spatula, stir egg-yolk mixture into chocolate mixture until blended. Wash and dry beaters.

• In separate large bowl, with clean beaters and with mixer at high speed, beat egg whites and cream of tartar until soft peaks form when beaters are lifted. With rubber spatula, gently fold beaten egg whites, one-third at a time, into chocolate mixture just until blended.

• Scrape batter into prepared pan; spread evenly. Bake 35 minutes. (Do not overbake; cake will firm upon standing and chilling.) Cool completely in pan on wire rack; refrigerate overnight in pan.

• Run thin knife, rinsed under very hot water and dried, around cake to loosen from side of pan; remove side of pan. Invert onto cake plate; unwrap foil from pan bottom and lift off pan. Carefully peel foil away from cake.

• To serve, let cake stand at room temperature 1 hour. Dust with confectioners' sugar. Or dust heavily with confectioners' sugar over paper doily or stencil.

Each serving: About 247 calories, 4g protein, 19g carbohydrate, 19g total fat (11g saturated), 120mg cholesterol, 125mg sodium.

Double-Chocolate Bundt Cake

PREP 30 MINUTES PLUS COOLING · BAKE 45 MINUTES · MAKES 20 SERVINGS

This lowfat cake will satisfy a chocolate craving. If you use a dusting of confectioners' sugar instead of the glaze, you'll save thirty-five calories per slice.

2¼	cups all-purpose flour
1½	teaspoons baking soda
½	teaspoon baking powder
½	teaspoon salt
¾	cup unsweetened cocoa
1	teaspoon instant espresso-coffee powder
¾	cup hot water
2	cups sugar
⅓	cup vegetable oil
2	large egg whites
1	large egg
1	square (1 ounce) unsweetened chocolate, melted
2	teaspoons vanilla extract
½	cup buttermilk
	Mocha Glaze (optional; recipe follows)

• Preheat oven to 350°F. Generously spray 12-cup Bundt pan with nonstick cooking spray.

• In medium bowl, combine flour, baking soda, baking powder, and salt.

• In measuring cup, whisk cocoa and espresso-coffee powder into hot water until blended.

• In large bowl, with mixer at low speed, beat sugar, oil, egg whites, and egg until blended. Increase speed to high; beat until creamy, about 2 minutes. Reduce speed to low; beat in cocoa mixture, melted chocolate, and vanilla until blended. Add flour mixture alternately with buttermilk, beginning and ending with flour mixture. Beat just until blended, occasionally scraping bowl with rubber spatula.

• Pour batter into prepared pan. Bake until toothpick inserted in center comes out clean, about 45 minutes. Cool cake in pan on wire rack 10 minutes. Run tip of knife around edge of cake to loosen from side of pan; invert onto rack to cool completely.

• Prepare Mocha Glaze, if you like. Pour over cooled cake.

> **Each serving without glaze:** About 185 calories, 3g protein, 34g carbohydrate, 5g total fat (1g saturated), 11mg cholesterol, 175mg sodium.
>
> **Each serving with glaze:** About 220 calories, 3g protein, 43g carbohydrate, 5g total fat (1g saturated), 11mg cholesterol, 175mg sodium.

Mocha Glaze

PREP 5 MINUTES   MAKES ABOUT 1 CUP

1/4   teaspoon instant espresso-coffee powder

2   tablespoons hot water

3   tablespoons unsweetened cocoa

3   tablespoons dark corn syrup

1   tablespoon coffee-flavored liqueur

1   cup confectioners' sugar

- In medium bowl, dissolve coffee powder in hot water. Stir in cocoa, corn syrup, and liqueur until blended. Stir in confectioners' sugar until smooth.

Each tablespoon: About 45 calories, 0g protein, 11g carbohydrate, 0g total fat (0g saturated), 0mg cholesterol, 5mg sodium.

Chocolate Soufflés

PREP 20 MINUTES PLUS COOLING   BAKE 25 MINUTES   MAKES 8 SERVINGS

Soufflés always make an impressive dessert. They are irresistible as individual soufflés and spectacular when baked as one large soufflé.

1 1/4	cups plus 3 tablespoons granulated sugar
2	tablespoons cornstarch
1	teaspoon instant espresso-coffee powder
1	cup milk
5	squares (5 ounces) unsweetened chocolate, chopped
3	tablespoons butter or margarine, softened
4	large eggs, separated
2	teaspoons vanilla extract
2	large egg whites
1/4	teaspoon salt
	confectioners' sugar

• In 3-quart saucepan, combine 1 1/4 cups granulated sugar, cornstarch, and espresso powder. With wire whisk, gradually stir in milk until blended. Cook over medium heat, stirring constantly, until mixture has thickened and boils; boil, stirring, 1 minute. Remove from heat.

• Stir in chocolate and butter until melted and smooth. With whisk, beat in egg yolks until well blended; stir in vanilla. Cool to lukewarm, stirring constantly.

• Meanwhile, preheat oven to 350°F. Grease eight 6-ounce custard cups or ramekins; sprinkle lightly with remaining 3 tablespoons granulated sugar.

• In large bowl, with mixer at high speed, beat 6 egg whites and salt just until stiff peaks form when beaters are lifted. Gently fold one-third of beaten egg whites into chocolate mixture; fold back into remaining egg whites just until blended.

• Spoon into prepared custard cups. Place in jelly-roll pan for easier handling. Bake until soufflés have puffed and centers are glossy, 25 to 30 minutes. (Add 10 minutes to baking time for large soufflé.) Dust with confectioners' sugar. Serve immediately.

Each serving: About 356 calories, 7g protein, 44g carbohydrate, 19g total fat (10g saturated), 122mg cholesterol, 178mg sodium.

Chocolate Cream Pie

Cream pies, as we know them today, have been popular in America for the last hundred years or so. If you prefer the piecrust to remain on the crisp side, serve the pie fairly soon after the filling has firmed up.

Chocolate Wafer–Crumb Crust (recipe follows)

3/4	cup sugar
1/3	cup cornstarch
1/2	teaspoon salt
3 3/4	cups milk
5	large egg yolks
3	squares (3 ounces) unsweetened chocolate, melted
2	tablespoons butter or margarine, cut into pieces
2	teaspoons vanilla extract
	Chocolate Curls (optional, recipe follows)
1	cup heavy or whipping cream

• Prepare crust as directed. Cool.

• Meanwhile, in heavy 3-quart saucepan, combine sugar, cornstarch, and salt; with wire whisk, stir in milk until smooth. Cook over medium heat, stirring constantly, until mixture has thickened and boils; boil 1 minute. In small bowl, with wire whisk, lightly beat egg yolks. Beat 1/2 cup hot milk mixture into beaten egg yolks. Slowly pour egg-yolk mixture back into milk mixture, stirring rapidly to prevent curdling. Cook over low heat, stirring constantly, until mixture is very thick or temperature on thermometer reaches 160°F.

• Remove saucepan from heat; stir in melted chocolate, butter, and vanilla until butter has melted and mixture is smooth. Pour hot chocolate filling into cooled crust; press plastic wrap onto surface. Refrigerate until filling is set, about 4 hours.

• Meanwhile, make Chocolate Curls, if using.

• To serve, in small bowl, with mixer at medium speed, beat cream until stiff peaks form; spoon over chocolate filling. Top with chocolate curls, if desired.

Chocolate Wafer–Crumb Crust

• Preheat oven to 375°F. In 9-inch pie plate, with fork, mix *1 1/4 cups chocolate-wafer crumbs (about 24 cookies), 4 tablespoons melted butter or margarine*, and *1 tablespoon sugar* until crumbs are evenly moistened. Press mixture firmly onto bottom and up side of pie plate, making small rim.

• Bake 10 minutes; cool on wire rack. Fill as recipe directs. Makes one 9-inch crust.

Chocolate Curls:

- Line a 5³/4" by 3 ¹/4" loaf pan with foil. In heavy 1-quart saucepan, combine *1 package (6 ounces) semisweet chocolate chips* and *2 tablespoons vegetable shortening*; heat over low heat, stirring frequently, until melted and smooth.

- Pour chocolate mixture into prepared pan. Refrigerate until chocolate is set, about 2 hours.

- Remove chocolate from pan by lifting edges of foil. Using vegetable peeler and working over waxed paper, draw blade across surface of chocolate to make large curls. If chocolate is too cold and curls break, let chocolate stand at room temperature until slightly softened, about 30 minutes. Use toothpick or wooden skewer to transfer for garnish.

Each serving: About 417 calories, 7g protein, 38g carbohydrate, 28g total fat (16g saturated), 171mg cholesterol, 329mg sodium.

Peanut Butter Swirl Brownies

PREP 30 MINUTES PLUS COOLING   BAKE 30 MINUTES   MAKES 24 BROWNIES

For the prettiest swirls, twist the knife just enough to create a bold pattern.

Brownie

1¹/₄ cups all-purpose flour

³/₄ teaspoon baking powder

¹/₂ teaspoon salt

¹/₂ cup butter or margarine (1 stick)

4 squares (4 ounces) unsweetened chocolate

4 squares (4 ounces) semisweet chocolate

1¹/₂ cups sugar

4 large eggs, lightly beaten

2 teaspoons vanilla extract

Peanut Butter Swirl

1 cup creamy peanut butter

4 tablespoons butter or margarine, softened

¹/₃ cup sugar

2 tablespoons all-purpose flour

1 large egg

1 teaspoon vanilla extract

• Preheat oven to 350°F. Grease 13" by 9" baking pan.

• Prepare Brownie: In small bowl, combine flour, baking powder, and salt. In 3-quart saucepan, melt butter and unsweetened and semisweet chocolates over low heat, stirring frequently, until smooth. Remove from heat; stir in sugar. Add eggs and vanilla; stir until well mixed. Stir flour mixture into chocolate mixture until blended.

• Prepare Peanut Butter Swirl: In medium bowl, with mixer at medium speed, beat peanut butter, butter, sugar, flour, egg, and vanilla until well blended.

• Spread 2 cups chocolate batter in pan; top with 6 large dollops of peanut butter mixture. Spoon remaining chocolate batter over and between peanut butter in 6 large dollops. With tip of knife, cut and twist through mixtures to create swirled effect.

• Bake until toothpick inserted 2 inches from edge comes out almost clean, 30 to 35 minutes. Cool in pan on wire rack.

• When cool, cut brownie lengthwise into 4 strips, then cut each strip crosswise into 6 pieces.

Each brownie: About 265 calories, 6g protein, 26g carbohydrate, 17g total fat (8g saturated), 61mg cholesterol, 185mg sodium.

Chocolate Truffle Tart

PREP 20 MINUTES PLUS CHILLING AND COOLING   BAKE 40 MINUTES   MAKES 12 SERVINGS

So unbelievably decadent, one thin slice is all you'll need.

Tart Pastry

1	cup all-purpose flour
1/4	teaspoon salt
6	tablespoons cold butter or margarine, cut into pieces
1	tablespoon vegetable shortening
2	to 3 tablespoons ice water

Chocolate Filling

6	squares (6 ounces) semisweet chocolate, coarsely chopped
1/2	cup butter or margarine (1 stick)
1/4	cup sugar
1	teaspoon vanilla extract
3	large eggs
1/2	cup heavy or whipping cream

softly whipped cream (optional)

White Chocolate Hearts
(optional; recipe follows)

- Prepare Tart Pastry: In large bowl, combine flour and salt. With pastry blender or two knives used scissor-fashion, cut in butter and shortening until mixture resembles coarse crumbs.

- Sprinkle in ice water, 1 tablespoon at a time, mixing lightly with a fork after each addition, until dough is just moist enough to hold together. Shape dough into disk; wrap in plastic wrap. Refrigerate 30 minutes or up to overnight. (If chilled overnight, let stand 30 minutes at room temperature before rolling.)

- Preheat oven to 425°F. On lightly floured surface, with floured rolling pin, roll dough into 11-inch round. Gently roll dough round onto rolling pin and ease dough into 9-inch tart pan with removable bottom. Fold overhang in and press dough against side of pan so it extends 1/8 inch above rim. Refrigerate or freeze until firm, 10 to 15 minutes.

- Line tart shell with foil; fill with pie weights or dry beans. Bake 15 minutes. Remove foil with weights; bake until golden, 5 to 10 minutes longer. If shell puffs up during baking, gently press it down with back of spoon. Cool in pan on wire rack. Turn oven control to 350°F.

- Meanwhile, prepare Chocolate Filling: In heavy 2-quart saucepan, melt chocolate and butter over very low heat, stirring frequently, until smooth. Add sugar and vanilla, stirring until sugar has dissolved. In small bowl, with wire whisk, lightly beat eggs and cream. Whisk 1/3 cup warm chocolate mixture into

egg mixture; stir egg mixture back into chocolate mixture in saucepan until blended.

• Pour warm chocolate filling into cooled tart shell. Bake until custard is set but center still jiggles slightly, about 20 minutes.

• Cool in pan on wire rack. When cool, carefully remove side of pan. Refrigerate until chilled, about 4 hours. Decorate with white chocolate hearts, or serve with whipped cream, if desired.

White Chocolate Hearts:

• With pencil, draw outline of 12 hearts, each about 1^1/$_2$" by 1^1/$_2$", on piece of waxed paper. Place waxed paper, pencil side down, on cookie sheet; tape to cookie sheet.

• In top of double boiler set over simmering water, melt *1^1/$_2$ ounces coarsely chopped white chocolate, Swiss confectionery bar,* or *white baking bar*, stirring, until smooth. Spoon warm chocolate into small pastry bag fitted with small writing tube; use to pipe heart-shaped outlines on waxed paper. Let hearts stand until set.

Each serving: About 306 calories, 4g protein, 22g carbohydrate, 24g total fat (14g saturated), 103mg cholesterol, 206mg sodium.

Whoopie Pies

You may remember these yummy treats from your childh
sandwiched with fluffy marshallow crème.

- 2 cups all-purpose flour

- 1 cup sugar

- 1/2 cup unsweetened cocoa

- 1 teaspoon baking soda

- 1/4 teaspoon salt

- 3/4 cup milk

- 6 tablespoons butter or margarine, melted

- 1 large egg

- 1 teaspoon vanilla extract

  Marshmallow Crème Filling
  (recipe follows)

- Preheat oven to 350°F. Grease 2 large cookie sheets.

- In large bowl, with wooden spoon, combine flour, sugar, cocoa, baking soda, and salt. Add milk, butter, egg, and vanilla; stir until smooth.

- Drop 12 heaping tablespoons batter, 2 inches apart, on each prepared cookie sheet.

- Bake until puffy a..
center comes out clean, 12 to .
rotating cookie sheets between upper a..
lower racks halfway through baking time. With wide spatula, transfer cookies to wire racks to cool completely.

- When cool, prepare Marshmallow Crème Filling. Spread 1 rounded tablespoon filling over flat side of 12 cookies. Top with remaining cookies, flat side down, to make 12 sandwiches.

Marshmallow Crème Filling

In large bowl, with mixer at medium speed, beat *6 tablespoons butter or margarine*, slightly softened, until creamy. With mixer at low speed, gradually beat in *1 cup confectioners' sugar* until blended. Beat in *1 jar (7 to 7 1/2-ounces) marshmallow crème* (about 1 1/2 cups) and *1 teaspoon vanilla extract* until well combined.

Each whoopie pie: About 360 calories, 4g protein, 60g carbohydrate, 13g total fat (8g saturated), 51mg cholesterol, 289mg sodium.

Chocolate Truffles

To add extra flavor to these easy-to-make bittersweet confections, stir two tablespoons of a favorite liqueur, such as Grand Marnier, or brandy into the melted chocolate mixture.

- 8 ounces bittersweet chocolate or 6 squares (6 ounces) semisweet chocolate plus 2 squares (2 ounces) unsweetened chocolate
- 1/2 cup heavy or whipping cream
- 3 tablespoons unsalted butter, cut into pieces and softened (do not use margarine)
- 1/3 cup hazelnuts (filberts), toasted and skinned (below), and finely chopped
- 3 tablespoons unsweetened cocoa

- Line 9" by 5" metal loaf pan with plastic wrap. In food processor with knife blade attached, process chocolate until finely ground.

- In 1-quart saucepan, heat cream to boiling over medium-high heat. Add cream to chocolate in food processor; process until smooth. Add butter; process to blend well.

- Pour chocolate mixture into prepared pan; spread evenly. Refrigerate until cool and firm enough to handle, about 3 hours.

- Place hazelnuts in small bowl, place cocoa in another small bowl. Remove chocolate mixture from pan by lifting edges of plastic wrap; invert chocolate block onto cutting board. Discard plastic. Cut chocolate block into 32 pieces. (To cut chocolate mixture easily, dip knife in hot water and wipe dry.) With cool hands, quickly roll each piece into a ball. One at a time, roll half of balls in hazelnuts and roll remaining balls in cocoa. Place in single layer in waxed paper–lined airtight container. Refrigerate up to 1 week or freeze up to 1 month. Remove from freezer 5 minutes before serving.

Toasting Nuts

Toasting nuts brings out their flavor, and in the case of nuts such as hazelnuts, allows the skins to be removed.

To toast almonds, pecans, walnuts, or hazelnuts, preheat the oven to 350°F. Spread the shelled nuts in a single layer on a cookie sheet. Bake, stirring occasionally, until lightly browned and fragrant, about 10 minutes. Toast hazelnuts until the skins begin to peel away. Let the nuts cool completely before chopping.

To skin hazelnuts, wrap the still-warm toasted nuts in a clean kitchen towel and let stand for about 10 minutes. Using the towel, rub off as much of the skins as possible (all of the skin may not come off).

Each truffle: About 65 calories, 1g protein, 5g carbohydrate, 6g total fat (3g saturated), 8mg cholesterol, 2mg sodium.

Creamy Fudge

PREP 10 MINUTES PLUS CHILLING   COOK 5 MINUTES   MAKES 64 PIECES

A silky smooth candy treat you can make up to one month ahead and freeze.

16	squares (16 ounces) semisweet chocolate, chopped
1	square (1 ounce) unsweetened chocolate, chopped
1	can (14 ounces) sweetened condensed milk
1¹/₂	teaspoons vanilla extract
¹/₈	teaspoon salt

• Line 8-inch square baking pan with foil, extending foil above rim of opposite sides.

• In 2-quart saucepan, combine semisweet and unsweetened chocolates and condensed milk. Cook, stirring constantly, over medium-low heat until chocolates have melted and mixture is smooth, about 5 minutes.

• Remove saucepan from heat; stir in vanilla and salt. Pour chocolate mixture into prepared pan; spread evenly. Refrigerate until firm, at least 4 hours or up to overnight.

• Remove fudge from pan by lifting edges of foil. Invert fudge onto cutting board; discard foil. Cut into 8 strips, then cut each strip crosswise into 8 pieces. Place pieces between waxed paper in airtight container. Store at room temperature up to 1 week, or refrigerate up to 1 month.

Chocolate-Walnut Fudge
Prepare as directed but stir in *1 cup walnuts (4 ounces)*, coarsely chopped, with vanilla and salt.

Each piece of Creamy Fudge: About 55 calories, 1g protein, 8g carbohydrate, 3g total fat (2g saturated), 2mg cholesterol, 15mg sodium.

Each piece of Chocolate-Walnut Fudge: About 67 calories, 1g protein, 8g carbohydrate, 4g total fat (2g saturated), 2mg cholesterol, 13mg sodium.

Rocky Road Ice Cream Cake

PREP 30 MINUTES PLUS CHILLING AND FREEZING   COOK 8 MINUTES   MAKES 14 SERVINGS

This ooey-gooey treat is like a big sundae made in a springform pan. It's prepared with chocolate ice cream, our secret Fudge Sauce (which is delicious spooned over a bowl of vanilla ice cream), cookies, peanuts, and miniature marshmallows. If you run short on time, jarred fudge sauce will do just fine.

Fudge Sauce

- 1   cup heavy or whipping cream
- 3/4   cup sugar
- 4   squares (4 ounces) unsweetened chocolate, chopped
- 2   tablespoons light corn syrup
- 2   tablespoons butter or margarine
- 2   teaspoons vanilla extract

Rocky Road Cake

- 2   pints chocolate ice cream, softened
- 14   chocolate sandwich cookies
- 2   cups miniature marshmallows
- 1   cup salted peanuts, coarsely chopped

• Prepare Fudge Sauce: In heavy 2-quart saucepan, combine cream, sugar, chocolate, and corn syrup. Heat to boiling over medium heat, stirring occasionally. Cook over medium-low heat, stirring constantly, until sauce thickens slightly, 4 minutes longer. Remove from heat. Add butter and vanilla; stir until butter has melted and sauce is smooth and glossy. Cover surface of sauce with plastic wrap; refrigerate until cool, about 2 hours. Makes about 1 2/3 cups.

• When sauce is cool, assemble Rocky Road Cake: Wrap outside of 9" by 3" springform pan with foil. Spoon 1 pint softened chocolate ice cream into pan. Cover ice cream with plastic wrap; press down to spread ice cream evenly and eliminate air pockets; remove plastic wrap. Insert cookies, upright, into ice cream to form a ring around side of pan, making sure to push cookie to pan bottom. Sprinkle 1 cup marshmallows and 1/2 cup peanuts over ice cream; gently press in with hand.

• Spoon remaining ice cream over marshmallows and peanuts. Place plastic wrap on ice cream and spread evenly; remove plastic. Spread 2/3 cup Fudge Sauce over ice cream (if sauce is too firm, microwave briefly to soften but do not reheat); reserve remaining sauce. Sprinkle remaining marshmallows and peanuts over sauce; press in gently with hand. Cover cake with plastic wrap and freeze until firm, at least 6 hours.

• To serve, uncover cake and remove foil. Wrap towels dampened with warm water around side of pan for about 20 seconds to slightly soften ice cream. Remove side of pan and place cake on cake stand or plate. Let stand at room temperature about 10 minutes for easier slicing. Meanwhile, place remaining Fudge Sauce in microwave-safe bowl. Heat in microwave oven, uncovered, on High 30 to 40 seconds or until hot, stirring once. Serve hot sauce to spoon over cake, if you like.

Each serving: About 365 calories, 7g protein, 36g carbohydrate, 23g total fat (11g saturated), 77mg cholesterol, 220mg sodium.

Brownie Sundae Cups

What could be better than brownie cupcakes filled with scoops of vanilla ice cream and driz-zled with fudge sauce. Both the brownies and sauce can be prepared hours ahead. Assemble the sundaes just before serving.

Brownie Cups

1	cup all-purpose flour
1/2	cup unsweetened cocoa
1	teaspoon baking powder
1/4	teaspoon salt
3/4	cup butter or margarine (1 1/2 sticks)
1 1/2	cups sugar
3	large eggs
2	teaspoons vanilla extract

Hot Fudge Sauce

1/2	cup sugar
1/3	cup unsweetened cocoa
1/4	cup heavy or whipping cream
2	tablespoons butter or margarine, cut in pieces
1	teaspoon vanilla extract
1	pint vanilla ice cream

• Preheat oven to 350°F. Grease 6 jumbo muffin-pan cups (about 4" by 2" each) or six 6-ounce custard cups.

• Prepare Brownie Cups: In medium bowl, combine flour, cocoa, baking powder, and salt. In 3-quart saucepan, melt butter over medium-low heat. Remove from heat; stir in sugar. Add eggs and vanilla; stir until well mixed. Stir in flour mixture just until blended. Spoon batter evenly into prepared muffin-pan cups.

• Bake until toothpick inserted in center comes out almost clean, 30 to 35 minutes. Cool in pan on wire rack 5 minutes. Run tip of thin knife around brownies to loosen from sides of pan. Invert brownies onto rack; cool 10 minutes longer to serve warm, or cool completely to serve later.

• While Brownie Cups are cooling, prepare Hot Fudge Sauce: In heavy 1-quart saucepan, combine sugar, cocoa, cream, and butter; heat to boiling over medium-high heat, stirring frequently. Remove from heat; stir in vanilla. Serve sauce warm, or cool completely, then cover and refrigerate up to 2 weeks. Gently reheat before using. Makes about 2/3 cup.

- Assemble brownie sundaes: With small knife, cut 1 1/2- to 2-inch circle in center of each brownie; remove tops and set aside. Scoop out brownie centers, making sure not to cut through bottoms of brownies. Transfer brownie centers to small bowl; reserve to sprinkle over ice cream another day. Place each Brownie Cup on dessert plate. Scoop ice cream into Brownie Cups and drizzle with Hot Fudge Sauce; replace brownie tops.

Each serving without sauce: About 500 calories, 7g protein, 61g carbohydrate, 28g total fat (16g saturated), 152mg cholesterol, 355mg sodium.

Each tablespoon fudge sauce: About 80 calories, 1g protein, 10g carbohydrate, 5g total fat (3g saturated), 14mg cholesterol, 25mg sodium.

Almond Cheesecake Brownies

PREP 30 MINUTES PLUS COOLING   BAKE 35 MINUTES   MAKES 24 BROWNIES

These sinfully rich brownies are marbled with a ribbon of cheesecake.

1¹/4	cups all-purpose flour
³/4	teaspoon baking powder
¹/2	teaspoon salt
¹/2	cup butter or margarine (1 stick)
4	squares (4 ounces) semisweet chocolate, chopped
4	squares (4 ounces) unsweetened chocolate, chopped
2	cups sugar
5	large eggs
2¹/2	teaspoons vanilla extract
1¹/2	packages (8 ounces each) cold cream cheese
³/4	teaspoon almond extract

• Preheat oven to 350°F. Grease 13" by 9" baking pan. In small bowl, combine flour, baking powder, and salt.

• In heavy 4-quart saucepan, melt butter and semisweet and unsweetened chocolates over low heat, stirring frequently, until smooth. Remove from heat. With wooden spoon, beat in 1¹/2 cups sugar. Add 4 eggs and 2 teaspoons vanilla; beat until well blended. Stir flour mixture into chocolate mixture just until blended.

• In small bowl, with mixer at medium speed, beat cream cheese until smooth; gradually beat in remaining ¹/2 cup sugar. Beat in remaining egg, almond extract, and remaining ¹/2 teaspoon vanilla just until blended.

• Spread 1¹/2 cups chocolate batter in prepared pan. Spoon cream-cheese mixture in 6 large dollops on top of chocolate mixture (cream-cheese mixture will cover most of chocolate batter). Spoon remaining chocolate batter over and between cream cheese in 6 large dollops. With tip of knife, cut and twist through mixtures to create marbled effect.

• Bake until toothpick inserted in center comes out almost clean, 35 to 40 minutes. Cool completely in pan on wire rack.

• When cool, cut brownie lengthwise into 4 strips, then cut each strip crosswise into 6 pieces.

Each brownie: About 238 calories, 4g protein, 26g carbohydrate, 14g total fat (8g saturated), 70mg cholesterol, 159mg sodium.

Metric Equivalents

The recipes that appear in this cookbook use the standard United States method for measuring liquid and dry or solid ingredients (teaspoons, tablespoons, and cups). The information on this chart is provided to help cooks outside the U.S. successfully use these recipes. All equivalents are approximate.

METRIC EQUIVALENTS FOR DIFFERENT TYPES OF INGREDIENTS

A standard cup measure of a dry or solid ingredient will vary in weight depending on the type of ingredient. A standard cup of liquid is the same volume for any type of liquid. Use the following chart when converting standard cup measures to grams (weight) or milliliters (volume).

Standard Cup	Fine Powder (e.g. flour)	Grain (e.g. rice)	Granular (e.g. sugar)	Liquid Solids (e.g. butter)	Liquid (e.g. milk)
1	140 g	150 g	190 g	200 g	240 ml
$^3/_4$	105 g	113 g	143 g	150 g	180 ml
$^2/_3$	93 g	100 g	125 g	133 g	160 ml
$^1/_2$	70 g	75 g	95 g	100 g	120 ml
$^1/_3$	47 g	50 g	63 g	67 g	80 ml
$^1/_4$	35 g	38 g	48 g	50 g	60 ml
$^1/_8$	18 g	19 g	24 g	25 g	30 ml

USEFUL EQUIVALENTS FOR LIQUID INGREDIENTS BY VOLUME

$^1/_4$ tsp	=				1 ml
$^1/_2$ tsp	=				2 ml
1 tsp	=				5 ml
3 tsp	=	1 tbls	=	$^1/_2$ fl oz	15 ml
	2 tbls	=	$^1/_8$ cup	1 fl oz	30 ml
	4 tbls	=	$^1/_4$ cup	2 fl oz	60 ml
	5$^1/_3$ tbls	=	$^1/_3$ cup	3 fl oz	80 ml
	8 tbls	=	$^1/_2$ cup	4 fl oz	120 ml
	10$^2/_3$ tbls	=	$^2/_3$ cup	5 fl oz	160 ml
	12 tbls	=	$^3/_4$ cup	6 fl oz	180 ml
	16 tbls	=	1 cup	8 fl oz	240 ml
	1 pt	=	2 cups	16 fl oz	480 ml
	1 qt	=	4 cups	32 fl oz	960 ml
				33 fl oz	1000 ml = 1 l

USEFUL EQUIVALENTS FOR DRY INGREDIENTS BY WEIGHT
(To convert ounces to grams, multiply the number of ounces by 30.)

1 oz	=	$^1/_{16}$ lb	=	30 g
4 oz	=	$^1/_4$ lb	=	120 g
8 oz	=	$^1/_2$ lb	=	240 g
12 oz	=	$^3/_4$ lb	=	360 g
16 oz	=	1 lb	=	480 g

USEFUL EQUIVALENTS FOR LENGTH
(To convert inches to centimeters, multiply the number of inches by 2.5.)

1 in	=		2.5 cm
6 in	=	$^1/_2$ ft =	15 cm
12 in	=	1 ft =	30 cm
36 in	=	3 ft = 1 yd =	90 cm
40 in	=		100 cm = 1 m

USEFUL EQUIVALENTS FOR COOKING/OVEN TEMPERATURES

	Fahrenheit	Celsius	Gas Mark
Freeze Water	32° F	0° C	
Room Temperature	68° F	20° C	
Boil Water	212° F	100° C	
Bake	325° F	160° C	3
	350° F	180° C	4
	375° F	190° C	5
	400° F	200° C	6
	425° F	220° C	7
	450° F	230° C	8
Broil			Grill